VANCOUVER

Text by
GIORGIO BIZZI

Photographs by
ANDREA PISTOLESI

ℬℬ
BONECHI

INDEX

Project and editorial conception: Casa Editrice Bonechi
Publication Manager: Monica Bonechi
Picture research: Monica Bonechi
Cover, Graphic design and Make-up: Manuela Ranfagni
Map: Stefano Benini - Firenze
Editing: Anna Baldini

Text: Giorgio Bizzi
English translation: Eve Leckey

© Copyright by Casa Editrice Bonechi - Florence - Italy
E-mail: bonechi@bonechi.it - Internet: www.bonechi.it

NEW YORK ADDRESS:
98 Thompson Street # 38 - New York, N.Y. 10012
Ph: (212) 343-9235 - Fax: (212) 625-9636
e-mail: bonechinyc@aol.com

Printed in Italy by Centro Stampa Editoriale Bonechi.

Photographs from archives of Casa Editrice Bonechi taken by
Andrea Pistolesi.

ISBN 88-8029-828-3

*   *   *

INTRODUCTION

An aerial view of **Vancouver**. To the right are the modern skyscrapers of **Downtown**. On the left is **False Creek** where the immense white teflon roof of **B.C. Place Stadium** is also visible.

Few cities are so immediately attractive that the casual visitor is actually tempted to move there permanently. Vancouver, according to its inhabitants, is one of those rare cities. It is quite normal to hear people who have been living there for only a few months already describing themselves as **Vancouverites** and quite a few tourists have gone straight from the hotel to the real estate agency determined to set up home there. Yet the city came into existence fairly recently if not exactly by pure chance, for strictly economic reasons. Indeed there is no record of any European presence in the area before 1774. That year a Spanish navigator, Juan Perez, exploring the land north of California, sailed around **Vancouver Island**, but there is no account of his landing there. It was **James Cook**, during one of his numerous voyages, who finally dropped anchor there in 1776 - though only to carry out necessary repairs. During this pause, however, the men under his command hunted otters, later selling their skins for a healthy profit in Macau.

This news did not fail to stimulate the curiousity of fur traders and hunters and Captain Cook, worried that the Spanish might send someone to claim the area from nearby California, sent Captain **George Vancouver** to map the coast and seek a northwest passage which would facilitate communications with the English colonies on the Atlantic coast. Vancouver completed his mission in 1792-93, but he did no more than give English names to the most important points of land, never dreaming that one day a lively, happy-go-lucky

3

city named after himself would be built there. The genial city of Vancouver had yet to be founded. In fact Cook decided to establish a landing point further to the south, at **New Westminster** and in 1793, Alexander McKenzie crossed Canada, opening up a route for fur hunting 400 kilometres further to the north than the spot where Vancouver was eventually founded. The rapid development of the area was caused instead by two vital factors: the discovery of gold in the **Fraser river** in 1858 and the interest of the Hudson Bay Company which moved into the area, exploiting the vast resources of wood and fur, and indeed administering it for 25 years. When the trans-Canadian railway was built in 1871 by **Canadian Pacific Railways**, in which the **Hudson Bay Company** had considerable shares, Vancouver was obviously considered to be the natural 'end of the line'.

Thus, with the completion of the railway in 1886 the city began to make its fortune. In the meantime, however, one of the most characteristic features of the city had come into being. **Gassy Jack's Saloon** opened in 1867 and became so important that in the 1970's a monument to its founder was unveiled on the original site.

The bar owed its renown to the fact that **Granville**, at the time a minor suburb of New Westminster, consisted of only a few timbermills processing the area's main resource (the discovery of gold did not lead to the 'fever' which had gripped California) without a single bar or inn. Thirsty labourers had to travel twenty kilometres if they wanted something stronger

*Downtown seen from the tranquil waters of **Coal Harbour**. The tower in the middle of the photo is the **Harbour Centre** at the top of which is a revolving restaurant.*

*A detail of one of the Indian **totems** at **Brockton Point** in **Stanley Park**.*

than water as the consumption of alcohol was forbidden near the timbermills. 'Gassy Jack' Deighton, so called for his endless ability to chatter, was well aware of the fact. With the help of some enthusiastic timber workers, the saloon was built in a single night and soon became the centre of a lively village named **Gastown** in Jack's honour. Today, despite the inevitable changes, Gastown forms the historic centre of the city of Vancouver and, after the extensive restoration work carried out during the 1970's, is also the most picturesque area. The railway also brought with it another most important contribution to the life of the city - the Chinese community. Here, as in California, a large number of Chinese worked on the building of the railway. Some had come north from the United States at the time of the gold rush in '58 though many more had immigrated directly from China. Their community grew rapidly and today it is second only to that of San Francisco. Although it is true to say that relations between the white community, mainly Anglo Saxon, and the Chinese have not always been easy in the past, the Chinese community is today one of the most active and prosperous in the city. Moreover, Vancouver is now one of the most important centres to attract investment, especially in the property market, from banks and wealthy private individuals in Hong Kong, given the imminent return of the British colony to the Republic of China. Indeed the recent building of skyscrapers in the city centre, mostly financed with money from Hong Kong, has provoked angry debate. In a city which has

*An aerial view of **False Creek** from above **Granville Island**, showing **Burrard Street Bridge** and **Granville Street Bridge**.*

Capilano Suspension Bridge, *a footbridge suspended 70 metres above the canyon.*

The **Granville Island Marina**, one of the best in
Vancouver. **Burrard Street Bridge** can be seen in the
background.

1,600,000 inhabitants spread over an area of 2,000 square kilometres, there seemed little need for sky-scrapers but, since the investors wished to recreate an image of the 'New Hong Kong', their buildings had to be metropolitan towers.

Another important characteristic of the city is the cli-mate. Vancouver is surrounded by the Coast Moun-tains, a continuation of the Cascade Range in the Unit-ed States, part of the North American Cordilleras sys-tem, which effectively shelter the city from the icy winds of the Canadian plains. The coast enjoys the mild effect of a warm current from Japan, and although the rain caused by the centre of high pressure over the Hawaii Islands gives Vancouver the reputation of being a very wet city, the rain is never torrential nor continu-al. Thus a mild micro-climate, very different to the rest of Canada, exists all year around.

With the mountains nearby, one can be on the ski slopes in only a few minutes from the city centre. In-deed, one of the local sayings is, "Vancouver is a city where you can ski in the morning, go sailing at lunchtime and play golf or tennis in the afternoon". Even if that is a bit too energetic for most, it is worth not-ing that the city has 25 private and public golf courses,

152 tennis courts and miles and miles of coast, bays and river for sailing, paddling a kayak or water skiing. From the economic point of view, the city is still one of the foremost producers of timber, paper and plastics, but this is now far from being the only source of wealth. The commercial port, known as the 'Gate to the East' or the 'Liverpool of Canada', became extremely important af-ter the opening of the Panama canal and now thrives with activity; another industry is provided by the ex-traction of natural gas which is abundant in the sur-rounding area; more recently there has been a boom in high technology businesses and services, splendidly represented during **Expo 1986**, and, though naturally overshadowed by Hollywood, there is a flourishing cin-ema and television industry. Add to all this a well-es-tablished and advanced social welfare system (in 1927 Vancouver and British Columbia were the first authori-ties in Canada to bring a pension scheme into being), and tight control over urban planning and private and public architectural initiatives and it is perhaps no sur-prise that present day Vancouver has been compared to San Francisco in the 1960's and '70's - a sort of Mec-ca for those who seek both a high standard in working conditions and a high-quality life style.

DOWNTOWN

COAL HARBOUR

Downtown Vancouver is on the eastern side of the peninsula which crosses Burrard Inlet, along which the city developed. and is centred around **Coal Harbour**, a natural port which formed the earliest landing point of the new city. Today Coal Harbour consists of several small tourist ports, such as the **Bay Shore Inn Marina,** opposite the busiest recreational centre in Downtown. Equipped with a swimming pool and sports centre, yachts can also be hired here to go cruising in small groups, or to take a fishing party to one of the magnificent inlets along the coast.

Burrard Inlet separates the centre from North and West Vancouver, but two bridges - **Lions Gate Bridge** and **Second Narrows Bridge** - link the areas and an efficient ferry service, the **Seabus**, plies back and forth continuously. On the Downtown side the terminal of both the Seabuses and the **Skytrain**, a modern elevated monorail, is in the historic **Canadian Pacific Railway Station,** built in 1912 to replace the original wooden station made in 1887 on completion of the trans-Canadian railway to which the city's history owes so much. As well as Coal Harbour, there is the commercial port which, with traffic of over 3,000 ships a year, is one of the most important on the North American Pacific coast. While goods ships dock on one shore of Burrard Inlet, mainly cruise boats berth on the other side, around Canada Place. These tourist cruises along the coasts of British Columbia and Alaska are both fascinating and unusual. Shorter trips of about four hours, around the peninsula, along the **Strait of Georgia** and around **English Bay**, can be made on one of the Harbour Ferries.

*Cruise ships anchored at **Canada Place** with the modern buildings of Downtown in the background.*

*On the following pages: a romantic view of Downtown at night, from **Coal Harbour** with the unmistakeable tower of the Harbour Centre in the middle.*

Canada Place extends along the seafront like a sailing ship at berth in the port of Vancouver.

A view of *Canada Place* with the modern buildings surrounding it and a detail of the 'sails'.

CANADA PLACE

Canada Place, one of the most famous architectural features of Vancouver, stands on what was once the historic *Pier B.C.*, the wharf belonging to the Canadian Pacific Railway where goods trains met the Pacific maritime traffic. The building was begun in 1983 and completed in 1986 to house the Canadian pavilion of the **Expo** held to celebrate the first centenary of the founding of Vancouver. As a reminder of the city's maritime history the building was designed to resemble a vast galleon with its sails spread wide. These five most original structures are in fact made of

fibreglass clad with teflon and are suspended from ten enormous steel 'masts', 25 metres in height. The overall effect is that of a gigantic ship in full sail. The maritime theme is further emphasized by the presence of luxurious cruise ships which berth here. At nightime, on special occasions, bright multi-coloured lights create fantastic effects on the translucent 'sails'. Inside, the building now houses the **World Trade Centre**, the **Vancouver Trade and Convention Centre**, and the **C.N. Imax Theatre** with a screen of more than 300 square metres which almost completely sur-

rounds the audience, drawing them into the documentaries, often three dimensional, which are shown there. On the top floor is the **Pan Pacific Hotel,** one of the most luxurious in Vancouver. The interior is entirely decorated in maplewood and pink marble which was sent to Italy for cutting and finishing. The various levels of Canada Place are linked by a glass elevator which provides a magnificent panoramic view. On the promenade along the wharf itself is a huge hall for passengers arriving and departing on cruises, as well as numerous shops and fast-food bars, many serving seafood specialities. Those who wish to eat in more elegant surroundings can visit the restaurants of the Pan Pacific Hotel or another, equally luxurious, at the further end of Canada Place. On a clear day, as well as the normal view of passing ships and hydrofoils (one of the most interesting means of transport in British Columbia) mooring and departing, one can enjoy a good view of **Mount Baker.** Three thousand metres above sea level, it was named after one of Captain Vancouver's officers and lies 80 kilometres south of the American border.

Multicoloured lights and the glow of the sunset reflect on the 'sails' of Canada Place.

*Cruise ships berthed in Canada Place. Cruises to the coastal ports of **British Columbia** and **Alaska** depart from here.*

*On the following pages: **Canada Place** adorned with lights at night-time.*

HARBOUR CENTRE

Not far from Canada Place, going towards the east, is the Harbour Centre, a tower which rises to a height of 169 metres, dominating the entire harbour area. The unusual mushroom-shaped **observation deck** at the top of the Harbour Centre is one of the best known features of the port and is visible from everywhere in the centre. From the panoramic terrace at the top, or seated comfortably at a table in the revolving restaurant, one can enjoy a magnificent view over all of Vancouver, the harbour and the bay. During the summer, the restaurant occasionally holds a 'theme evening' based entirely on salmon, demonstrating the incredible variety of ways in which this delicious fish may be cooked and served. There is also a multimedia presentation on the beauties of Vancouver, designed for tourists but extremely informative, which lasts 15 minutes.

*The **Harbour Centre Observation Deck**, at a height of 169 metres. The entire city is visible from the revolving restaurant.*

*The **Harbour Centre** towers over the other buildings in the area of the port.*

*The elaborate decorations of the **Marine Building** at 355 Burrard Street.*

*The Art Déco **Marine Building**, once the tallest in Vancouver, reflected on the glass façade of a more modern structure nearby.*

THE MARINE BUILDING

At number **355 Burrard Street**, on the corner with **Hastings Street**, is the Marine Building, an elegant and varied structure climbing up to a single pinnacle. Its designers, McCarter and Nairne wrote of it, "...it is like a rock, rising from the sea, covered with marine flora and fauna...and dusted with gold". Built in **Art Déco** style in 1929, it is one of the most famous buildings in the city. At the time of its construction, it was also the tallest building in Vancouver. Now restored, it stands amidst the modern, towering skyscrapers as evidence of Vancouver's early expansion, dramatically interrupted by the Depression of the 1930's. The **elaborate decorative detail of the vestibule** and the elegant stained glass windows are quite magnificent.

*Separated by only a few metres, the Neoclassic **Art Gallery** and the modern style of the **Law Courts** manage to blend happily in Vancouver.*

*The many different architectural styles of Robson Square. On the left is the vast Neogothic **Hotel Vancouver.***

VANCOUVER ART GALLERY

The Vancouver Art Gallery is housed in what was originally the old courthouse of British Columbia. A Neoclassic building dated 1909, it was designed by Francis Rattenbury, the same architect who designed the Parliament Buildings of British Columbia and the Empress Hotel, the two most famous buildings in Victoria. The gallery opened in 1931 and houses works of art by many Canadian and international artists as well as the most important collection of works by Emily Carr, the best known British Columbian artist; it also provides research and educational facilities for students. The building is on the north side of Robson Square and immediately behind it on the left is one of the most elegant buildings in the city: the **Hotel Vancouver**. This impressive Neo-gothic building was begun in 1929 but the Depression caused work to stop almost immediately. It was only completed some ten years later on the occasion of the visit of King George VI and Queen Elizabeth.

THE LAW COURTS

From an architectural point of view, the entire area around Robson Square is of interest, but the **Law Courts** are particularly famous. On the south side of the square, this building of metal and glass was designed by Arthur Erikson and is one of the most impressive in the centre. Opened in 1979, its unusual design, despite its apparent stolidity, contains an extremely versatile arrangement of space, housing not only the civil and penal courts of British Columbia, but also the archives and many other public offices. The entire structure, which faces onto both Howe Street and Hornby Street, slopes down towards Robson Square in an imaginative series of steps and chutes with flowing water.

ROBSON SQUARE

Robson Square is an entirely pedestrian zone and is Vancouver's most **popular meeting place**, rather like Rockefeller Plaza in New York. The square is built on several levels: on the lowest, beneath street level, are shops, restaurants and cafés which arrange their tables outside during the summertime making the square even more lively and colourful. This level is partially covered by domes made of dark glass and metal, contrasting with the Neoclassic style of the Art Gallery, but blending with the modern design of the Law Courts. In summer, the gardens on the upper level are a favourite spot at lunchtime for those shopping or working in the centre, while in the wintertime, just like its counterpart in New York, it becomes a popular ice-skating rink.

*Busy night-time traffic on **Robson Street***.

(Clockwise): elegant shops, a bird's-eye view of Robson Street and two typical shop signs in the street.

ROBSON STREET

Once known as **Robsonstrasse** due to the large number of German restaurants which had sprung up there, some of which have survived until today, and the delicatessen shops and elegant patisseries which lent it a distinctly European flavour, today this is the street of designer fashion. The image is now more that of Rodeo Drive in Beverley Hills where the stars shop, than Via Montenapoleone in Milan or other similar streets in European cities.

Yet most of the fashion names adorning the stylish shop windows are, indeed, European, especially Italian, while signs in bars invite you to have an espresso or cappuccino. The numerous restaurants along Robson Street have that unmistakeable cosmopolitan air which one finds in all large cities. Here there is something for everyone, from Japanese sushi to vegetarian specialities, from Mexican chile to Californian cuisine, which now seems more pop-

ular in British Columbia than in California. Thus Robson Street, with its cultural mix and the lively assortment of bypassers, is a prime example of Vancouver's multi-ethnic character and the love of life which have earned the city its reputation as **lucky** or even **lazy**.

At night, during the weekends, there is an intense traffic of cars along Robson Street either heading for the many nightclubs in the area or simply cruising along the pavement in search of company. The local police have often tried to impose a block on traffic, but have always come up against the opposition of businessmen who, faced with astronomical rents in the most elegant downtown street, keep their shops and premises open day and night. At the far end of the street, to the west, is Robson Market, a modern covered market where all kinds of fresh produce can be bought.

*Vancouver's modern 'Colosseum', the **New Library**,*
opened in 1995.

THE NEW LIBRARY

Vancouver's new public library cost one hundred million dollars and opened in 1995. It lies on the west side of the area known as the Robson Strip, one of the newer districts of the city. Inspired by the **Colosseum** in Rome as it stands today, the building is as elegant and varied as it is intriguing.

Built of pink stone, the rooms inside are perfectly lit by the enormous glass windows which, due to the circular design of the building, provide direct light at all hours of the day.

The library is on Robson Street at the junction with Homer Street and represents a distinct change in atmosphere from the colourful, fashionable area to the lively cultural life of Vancouver.

*The classic design of the **cathedral** stands out among the modern steel and glass buildings of Downtown.*

*The **Cenotaph**, in **Victory Square** park, to the memory of those who died in the First World War.*

CATHEDRAL SQUARE AND VICTORY SQUARE

In the days when the Downtown area was still covered by thick forest, the bishop of the young city pointed to the highest tree and quite simply said, ''There, build it there''. Today the **Holy Rosary Cathedral** (1900) stands in one of the Vancouverites favourite squares . **Victory Square**, just off Hastings Street between Cambie and Hamilton Street, has one of the few parks in Downtown. The courthouse, the first important building to be constructed outside **Gastown**, was originally here. After the great fire of 1886 it became a public square and, after the courthouse had been demolished, it was used for recruiting troops for the First World War. The **Cenotaph** was built here in 1924 to commemorate those who died in that war.

GASTOWN

THE STEAM CLOCK

One of the most popular sights in Gastown, the old centre of Vancouver, stands on the corner between Cambie and Water Street. An intriguing clock, driven by a steam mechanism, draws the crowds here. Made in 1977 by clockmaker Ray Saunders, the steam clock is driven by a mechanism designed in 1875, the workings of which are visible inside the glass and bronze structure. Every hour the steam, from an underground system, sets off a series of whistles while a music box inside the clock plays the chimes of **Big Ben** every quarter of an hour. The steam clock is symbolic of the revival which took place in Gastown in the 1970's when a restoration programme saved it from decline and destruction. It is now a lively district which attracts the young and, with its antique shops, art galleries, cafés and restaurants, the area has a relaxed, bohemian atmosphere.

*Clouds of steam from the whistles of the **steam clock** which blow every hour. The complex mechanism is visible inside.*

*Picturesque **Water Street** in the heart of old Gastown with the modern **Harbour Centre** in the background.*

*The statue to **Gassy Jack**, the innkeeper reputed to have founded **Gastown**.*

*The sign of **Gaolers Mews** is a reminder of the first prison in riotous old Gastown.*

GASSY JACK

In **Maple Tree Square**, where the first elections were held under a tree, is a statue to 'Gassy Jack' the hero who gave his name to the early pioneering town, standing on a barrel of the whisky he sold. At the point where Gassy Jack's saloon stood, on the corner of Carrol Street and Water Street, the division of Vancouver into civic zones begins.

GAOLERS MEWS

In the early days Gastown was not exactly a peaceful place to live and some of the street names reflect its turbulent past, such as **Blood Alley** and **Gaolers Mews**.
Here, on the spot where Vancouver's very first police station once stood, today there is a brick-paved courtyard surrounded by walls covered with creepers and ivys.

WATER STREET

Water Street, beginning at the **steam clock** and ending at the statue to **Gassy Jack** on the corner of Carrol Street, is the livliest street in Gastown. Attractively paved and lined with trees on both sides, it is crowded with cafés and restaurants where it is pleasant to sit at tables outside on sunny days.

CHINATOWN

Pavements crowded until late at night, brightly coloured neon lights, constant traffic jams: this is a city within a city and an important part of Vancouver's history. **Chinatown** is one of the oldest districts in the city. The Chinese community began to settle here at the time of the gold rush around 1858 and later increased as workers, hired to build the railway, arrived and, with the continual flow of immigrants, has now reached one hundred thousand members. Despite frequent conflicts in the past - between 1878 and 1913 many anti-Chinese laws were passed and the right to vote was only conceded in 1947 - the business life of Chinatown prospered. The first president of China, Sun-Yat-Sen came here in 1911 to collect funds for the Kuomintang and the **Dr. Sun-Yat-Sen-Park**, a magnificent garden in Ming style, is dedicated to him. At the entrance to the area in **Pender Street** is the **Chinese Cultural Centre**, the most important symbol of Chinatown's identity. The entire area is now considered a national monument comprising such buildings as that of the **Chinese Benevolent Association** (1909), the **Sam Kee Building**, mentioned in the Guinness Book of Records as the narrowest building in the world (2 metres wide), the **Wing Sang Building**, the oldest, dating from 1889, and many others of interest.

In the local shops you can buy all manner of specialities from foodstuffs to antique porcelain. If you happen to visit Chinatown around January or February (the date varies depending on the lunar calendar) you may see the colourful **Chinese New Year** celebrations which last from three days to a week.

*Scenes in the **Dr. Sun-Yat-Sen Park**, opened in 1986.*

*A detail of the entrance to the **Chinese Pavilion** made for Expo '86, now in Chinatown; a display of Chinese delicacies; banners and lanterns to celebrate the **Chinese New Year**.*

*On the following pages: the entrance to the **Chinese Pavilion**.*

STANLEY PARK

THE TOTEM POLES

Stanley Park, covering an area of 405 hectares, the entire tip of the peninsula crossing the end of Burrard Inlet, is one of the largest in the world. Vancouver is rightly proud of this feature which not only contributes to the city's much renowned quality of life, but is also a reminder of the primitive natural paradise which the first European settlers found. Although the park is constantly maintained and has been carefully designed, creating recreational areas suited to all kinds of different sports, the central section has been left entirely in the natural state.

The American Indians lived in this paradise and the Squamish tribe still lived here in the Khwaykhway village at the time of its designation as a civic park. Lord Stanley, the governor who opened the park on 27 September 1889, dedicated it to "...the use and enjoyment of people of all creeds, colours and customs, for ever". **Totem poles** belonging to all the tribes who lived along the coast were placed at **Brockton Point** during the 1920's. Nearby, cricket and rugby are played on the **Oval Sports Field.**

For each individual Indian tribe the totem pole is not unlike the emblem of an ancient family in Europe. They represent the stylized, brightly coloured figures of the animal gods which make up the complex American Indian religion, such as the Crow with the large beak, the Wolf, the Fox, the Beaver, the Eagle, the Whale and the legendary **Thunderbird**, with its wings spread, the god of thunder, lightning and rain. From Stanley Park a road bridge crosses a narrow stretch of road to **Deadman's Island**, where there is an ancient Indian cemetry.

*Here and on the following pages, the **totem poles** in **Stanley Park**. The details show the stylized images of the gods, incarnated as various animals.*

*Through the glass panels of the **Canadian Arctic Gallery** visitors can observe large mammals of the polar seas at close quarters.*

*The **beluga** is one of the most gentle and unusual sea creatures. Also known as the 'sea canary' due to the incredible range of noises it can produce, it is one of the most popular animals in the **Vancouver Aquarium**.*

*The real star of the Aquarium is the whale. It performs amazing acrobatics in the enormous pool, capable of holding **2 million litres of water**, and is one of the most popular attractions for visitors who crowd around the pool every day to watch.*

THE AQUARIUM

The Vancouver Aquarium opened in 1956 and was the first aquarium open to the public in Canada. With subsequent developments and extensions it has become the foremost and the largest in the country and one of the biggest in all of North America, visited by 800,000 people every year. More than 570 species are kept here, with over 8,000 animals ranging from fish to aquatic mammals, from invertebrates to amphibians, from snakes to birds. The aquarium is run by an independent, non profit-making organization whose main purpose is to educate school and organized groups concerning the importance of marine life. Various ecosystems have been recreated in various sections within the aquarium. One of the most recent, opened by Queen Elizabeth II in 1983, is dedicated to the **Amazonian Rain Forest** and houses piranha, anaconda, marbled ray fish, slath and birds. Another section perfectly reproduces the environment of the **Tropical Pacific** with the coral reefs of the Hawaii Islands and Australia, complete with sharks. The **Bunaken National Marine Park** of Indonesia is also recreated with its brilliantly coloured fish, while yet another section is devoted to tropical environments in various parts of the world and includes both salt and fresh-water species from Florida, the Philippines, Mexico, Fiji, and the Red Sea. However, the largest section is obviously that representing the coasts of **British Columbia** and the **Canadian Arctic**. Firstly, the coastal environment of the North Pacific has been recreated including a colony of otters, born in captvity in the aquarium, seals, numerous species of fish native to cold water zones, and even the less spectacular but just as important details such as outcrops of algae and plankton. The second part of this section, however, provides the greatest attraction of the entire aquarium: here, hundreds of spectators crowd around the sides of an enormous pool which cost ten million dollars and holds two million litres of water, to watch the games of the whales and dolphins as they play and leap only an arm's length away. It would be quite unjust to think that the owners of the aquarium have organized a 'show', for the awe-in-

spiring whales and the dolphins are not in the least trained or incited to put on any kind of circus performance. These enormous creatures are rightly defined as being 'playful' because of their evident pleasure in games, leaps and pirouettes and their 'non-economic' behaviour which has an entirely communicative purpose. Indeed, their acrobatic leaps out of the water, sometimes even to a height of several metres, are simply part of their natural behaviour which is so extremely sociable that amazed and less spontaneous humans consider it to be 'spectacular'. These mammals are so free and at ease in the environment which has been exactly recreated for them down to the smallest detail, that one may even hear them speaking to each other with their strange, shrill cries, so intensely expressive that they must surely be defined as a real language. So important are the whales and dolphins for the aquarium, and so popular are they with the public, that a bronze statue by the Canadian artist, **Bill Reid**, is dedicated to them at the building's entrance. This sculptor, of American Indian origin, is famous for having studied and reintroduced the traditional techniques used by the Indians in carving totem poles, and he also directed the reconstruction of a village of the Haida tribe, to which his mother belonged, in Vancouver's Museum of Anthropology.

In a magnificent gallery with glass panels at the lower level of the pool, visitors can observe every detail of the underwater life of these huge marine mammals, study their behaviour and biology more closely and almost rub noses with the enormous, gentle **beluga,** a type of whale quite common in Arctic waters. The beluga, noted for its slightly comic and affectionate expression, is also known as the **sea canary**, due to the wide range of sounds it is capable of reproducing. The aquarium also supports many research programmes throughout the world and is involved in the care and rehabilitation of animals ranging from reptiles to marine mammals and as a result of both this and of its normal activities and programmes, is now internationally renowned as one of the foremost scientific organizations in its field.

The marine mammals are completely at ease in the recreated habitat of the **North Pacific Coast***, and even manage to reproduce here.*

A beluga playing in the **Canadian Arctic Gallery***.*

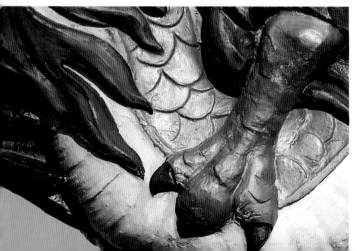

*The **figure-head** of the **Empress of Japan** and two details of the design.*

THE SS EMPRESS OF JAPAN

Vancouver owes its initial development to the **Canadian Pacific Railway Company** which effectively governed the area for many years and still links the city to the rest of Canada. The company also created a fleet of merchant ships which contributed considerably to economic expansion into the Pacific. Between 1891 and 1922, the fleet had several Empress class ships. The name **Empress** derived from the title of Empress of India assumed by Queen Victoria in 1876 (a luxury hotel in Victoria, the main city of Vancouver Island, bears the same name). According to the route covered by a ship, the name of a country was added to that of the class.

Today, a plexiglass reproduction of the figure-head of one of those ships, the **Empress of Japan**, facing out to sea near the aquarium, is a reminder of those heroic days when Vancouver first began to expand.

THE WET SUIT GIRL

When the Wet Suit Girl, a bronze statue by Elek Imredy representing a girl in a bathing suit sitting on a rock by the sea, was unveiled just past **Brockton Point** near **Lions Gate Bridge** in 1970, she was greeted by uproar from the critics who judged her as banal and silly. Others, happier to see their flourishing young city attractively adorned, especially if there were similarities to the monuments of older and more famous cities, saw in her a Canadian version of Copenhagan's famous *Mermaid*. The **Vancouver Harbour Improvement Society** which had donated the statue to the city, cut short the discussion by stating that the image of the young girl was symbolic of the exploration of the Canadian continental shelf (as witnessed by the flippers on her feet). Despite the polemics, the Wet Suit Girl is one of the most popular decorative elements in Vancouver today.

*The **'wet suit girl'** looks as though she is ready to dive into the sea.*

SPORT AND THE STATUE TO JEROME

Vancouver happily combines the natural tendency towards physical exercise inherited from a pioneering past with the recent mania for health and fitness. Favoured by the climate and position, every day thousands of citizens can be seen enthusiastically playing cricket or rugby matches, golf, riding bicycles or racing (the **Tour of Gastown** is an urban circuit open to all), sailing or canoe racing, downhill skiing or climbing, going on kayak trips or taking part in most unusual amateur sporting activites, such as the **bath-tub race**, a competition in which baths, fitted with outboard motors, speed along the 61 kilometres of the Strait of Georgia. From so many sportsmen, champions are sure to emerge. A statue commemorates one of these, **Harry Jerome**, the "fastest man in the world" in track events.

Even the very youngest Vancouverites love the open-air life.

*The statue to **Harry Jerome**, "the fastest man in the world".*

The lighthouse at **Brockton Point** *and a view of* **Lions Gate Bridge** *from* **Prospect Point**.

BROCKTON POINT

At the eastern end of Stanley Park, at **Brockton Point**, stands an old lighthouse from where all the traffic of Burrard Inlet can be controlled. Nearby is the **Nine O'Clock Gun**, a cannon which was once fired at six in the afternoon to signal the suspension of all fishing. The firing of the shot is now postponed to nine in the evening.

PROSPECT POINT

From the look-out of Prospect Point at the most northerly end of Stanley Park one can enjoy not only the scene of boats and ships passing beneath **Lions Gate Bridge** as they enter and leave Burrard Inlet, but also a wonderful view of the mountains on the **North Shore**. A monument here commemorates the *Beaver*, Vancouver's first steam ship, which capsized on the rocks opposite the viewpoint in 1888.

Lions Gate Bridge crosses Burrard Inlet at First Narrows.

Ships of any size can pass under the bridge which is 60 metres high.

The suspension bridge can carry intense traffic on its three lanes.

LIONS GATE BRIDGE

Lions Gate Bridge was built at **First Narrows**, the narrowest point across Burrard Inlet. A suspension bridge just under two kilometres in length, it is 60 metres high at the centre to allow the largest ships to pass beneath. It was opened in 1938 after bitter opposition from Vancouver's administrators who feared it would damage the unspoilt beauty of Stanley Park. The southern entrance to the bridge is guarded by two stone lions sculpted by Charles Marega, who was born in Trieste. Building was financed by a group of English investors, headed by the Guinness family, who intended to facilitate the development of properties which they owned in the upper part of **West Vancouver**, now known as the **British Properties**.

The spectacular fireworks which close the
Vancouver Sea Festival.

THE FIREWORKS

The **Vancouver Sea Festival** is held every July. Based in **English Bay** on the western side of Stanley Park, this summer festival is a lively whirl of activities and celebrations including immense barbecues of salmon on the beach, acrobatic displays of First World War biplanes, bath-tub races in the bay, music, dancing (the **Vancouver Folk Festival** with Canadian and American singers is held on **Jerico Beach**) and a gigantic firework display to end the festivities. The fireworks are set off from a barge anchored in the bay and light up the entire area with a magical array of exploding colour which is visible from even the furthest corners of Vancouver.

THE WEST END

In the days when the **Canadian Pacific Railway** was still in its pioneering stage, the officials of the railway chose the **West End**, the area overlooking **English Bay**, south of Stanley Park and west of Downtown, to build their residences. Here, far from the alcoholic binges and riotous behaviour so common in Gastown and from the resented Chinese community, they built an elegant, English-style suburb. Vancouver was therefore divided into three sections which rigidly respected the class and ethnic divisions so typical of 19th-century society. Up until 1955, the area more or less maintained this aspect, with only one building, the **Hotel Sylvia**, which could be described as 'tall' with its mere eight stories.

Today instead, it is the foremost residential area and the most densely populated in Vancouver with some 50,000 inhabitants in an area of only 7.7 square kilo-metres. The population, consisting of all kinds of ethnic groups, lives in comfortable multi-storey condominiums with family villas nestling below like the undergrowth of a forest of skyscrapers. Recently many streets in the West End have been closed to traffic making the area more pleasant to live in. In addition, due to its position in the centre of the city, it is popular with single people, both old and young, artists and those who do not need a great deal of space or who may live there only briefly. Consequently the neighbourhood is continually changing and very lively.

The shops on **Robson, Denman** and **Davie Streets** reflect this genuine multi-ethnic atmosphere; small and varied and set amidst a series of little squares with trees, flowers and benches, the West End seems more like a small European city than a Northern American metropolis.

*Tall blocks of apartments in the **West End** look across **English Bay** crowded with merchant ships and pleasure craft.*

ENGLISH BAY

English Bay lies between Stanley Park and the peninsula which divides Burrard Inlet from the Strait of Georgia.

All day long fishing and pleasure boats, as well as ships heading towards the harbour wharfs on the other side of Lions Gate Bridge, ply across the bay. Lying just behind English Bay is the **West End** and consequently the beach here is very popular with those who live in the city centre. People of all ages jog and cycle along the seafront in the fresh ocean breeze. In the summertime one can relax in the sun on the beach just a few yards from home, while the sea is dotted with the brightly coloured sails of windsurfers. On New Year's Day, thousands of participants take part in the **Polar Bear Swim**. Not for the flight of heart, people rush into the chilly waters of the Pacific just to say they did it. In the summer, the area comes alive with the annual **Sea Festival** featuring street performers and casual entertainment.

For Vancouverites - and their four-legged friends - **English Bay** *is an ideal place for relaxation and recreation, while groups of musicians find a ready audience. The police keep a discreet eye on things.*

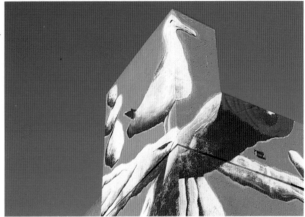

Bogart, Groucho Marx and the Little Mermaid are portrayed seated in a cinema on a wall mural - a reminder that Vancouver is a new centre for the cinema industry.

*Crowds of pedestrians in **Denman Street** as they visit the attractive small shops.*

An unusual trompe-l'oeil gives a marine flavour to one of the shop signs.

DENMAN STREET

Many of the streets in Vancouver have a rather **European atmosphere**, but Denman Street is perhaps the most authentic of all. Little shops smelling of wonderful spices from all over the world, ethnic specialities, tiny boutiques with low prices and original clothing, restaurants and cafés with tables outside where people chat freely to each other, clubs where, as well as good food, you will find excellent live jazz, kiosks and stalls which serve the most varied styles of cuisine in fast-food form, alternate along the pavement, indicated by bright, original signs. On summer evenings the street is closed to traffic, and becomes an open-air salon. Often the bars and restaurants advertise themselves with unusual and amusing billboards set out in the street with such surprising descriptions and statements as "The bar with the headwaiter straight out of hell," or "Our speciality is insults": a typical example of Vancouver's youthful liveliness and the happy tendency to take life light-heartedly.

Roedde House in the old part of Vancouver, with modern skyscrapers in the background.

*The **Victorian-Edwardian style** has been perfectly reproduced in the sitting-room, down to the smallest detail.*

ROEDDE HOUSE MUSEUM

A city which has existed for barely one hundred years naturally tends to think that any building or item which is even slightly old represents an important part of its history, and rightly so. Thus the house of **Gustav Roedde**, the very first bookbinder in Vancouver, has been made into a museum. The house, built in 1893, is a typical example of a 19th-century West End residence. The interior is decorated with original Victorian and Edwardian furnishings, collected and arranged by the **Roedde House Preservation Society**, an organization which was founded in 1984.
Another nine buildings, dating from 1890 to 1908 in the same area form the **Barclay Heritage Square**, a sort of 'archaeological park' portraying various aspects of the original West End.

GRANVILLE ISLAND

BRIDGES RESTAURANT

Granville Island is not a real island. It was made in 1916 by the backfill produced when dragging **False Creek**, the stretch of sea which separates the southern and central areas of the city and is actually attached to the south bank by a narrow strip of land. Until the 1950's, Vancouver's largest industrial plants were here. As these industries declined, the area was gradually abandoned until 1973 when a reclamation programme began, turning the area into one of the busiest in the city. One of the most convenient, and certainly the most picturesque, ways of reaching the island from the centre is to take a **mini-ferry**, one of the cute little boats which ply back and forth across False Creek continuously from 8 in the morning until 8 in the evening. Where once industrial warehouses stood along the wharfs, today there are cafés and restaurants with tables outside, directly overlooking the ships and boats, giving visitors a real feeling of seafaring life. Between the two bridges of **Burrard** and **Granville Street**, **Bridges Restaurant** stands out entirely painted bright yellow. This is, perhaps, Vancouver's most fashionable restaurant, where locals like to bring visiting friends to try the renowned seafood cooking. Tables, shaded by large yellow umbrellas, are spread over the whole wharf where one of the two ferry companies berths. In the winter months instead, one can enjoy the romantic sight of the harbour with yachts covered with snow, from the vast windows of Bridges Restaurant.

*The small harbour of **Granville Island** on **False Creek**, crowded with yachts. In the background is **Burrard Street Bridge**.*

*On the wharf of **Bridges Restaurant**, excellent fish and seafood are served outside, right in the heart of the port itself.*

*On the following pages: a view of **Granville Island** from **Granville Street Bridge**. On the right is the **Public Market**.*

*The **Marina** on Granville Island provides excellent mooring for yachts close to the city's modern apartment blocks.*

THE MARINA

The protected waters of **False Creek** between the southwest side of **Granville Island** and **Burrard Street Bridge** are ideal for sheltering small craft. One of the main tourist ports of Vancouver, the Granville Island **Marina**, has therefore been created here. Consisting of a series of handy floating landing stages, the little harbour provides convenient permanent berthing for yachts and motor boats during both the summer and winter months, almost in the centre of the city itself. Vancouver, in fact, is the only Canadian port not to freeze over in the winter and, if the sea and weather conditions are suitable, one can often see a boat set sail from here even in mid-winter, covered with snow.

Vancouverites love the sea and sailing so much that they simply never miss a chance.

Many of these boats, most of which are small, though there are also large motor vessels for open sea trips, offer a charter service and may be rented for a fishing trip or for a cruise along the coast or around **Vancouver harbour**. Anyone who wants to enjoy a bit of physical activity, or just wander around False Creek can easily find a small rowing boat, kayak or windsurfer to rent.

Those who arrive in the port by sea are entitled to three hours free berthing, just long enough to try the specialities of the restaurants in the area.

The port is also well equipped with everything necessary for yachts and sailing: there are workshops, equipment for towing and launching, shops for spare parts and rigging, as well as stores and banks. The combination of this and the restaurants, theatres, crafts shops and artists' studios on Granville Island, give the area the unique and fascinating atmosphere of both a practical working port with, however, a sophisticated, cosmopolitan flavour.

The sign of the **Maritime Market** is a surf board. Kayaks are neatly stacked outside.

THE MARITIME MARKET

In the area in front of the wharfs of the tourist port, in a large and magnificently restored warehouse, is the **Maritime Market**. In this commercial centre all the equipment necessary on board can be bought: anchors, ropes, radios, fenders, everything from suitable clothing to inflatable life boats. The kayaks, attractively and neatly stacked into their racks outside the market, are also available for hire, while inside one can obtain information on yachts available for chartering. As now seems to happen in tourist ports everywhere, the Maritime Market is not only frequented by seasoned sailors, but also by landlubbers who come to buy the latest high-tech clothing which has recently become fashionable for less demanding uses than those originally intended.

GRANVILLE STREET BRIDGE

Once connected to the south side of Vancouver by a smaller bridge, **Old Bridge**, Granville Island is now linked to the city's road system by **Granville Street Bridge**, a road bridge which crosses right over the island. An exit from the bridge for traffic coming from the south side of False Creek and from the centre leads to **Anderson Street** and thus to Granville Street. However, the main purpose of the bridge is not to provide access to Granville Island which not only is too small to cope with much traffic but also has very limited parking. Rather, the bridge relieves **Burrard Street Bridge**, leading to the residential West End, of some traffic and directs it towards the larger arterial roads and motorways. Crossing over the bridge, there is a magnificent view of Granville Island below.

*Large apartment blocks on the other side of **False Creek** seen from Granville Street Bridge.*

***Granville Street Bridge** crossing False Creek.*

*The entrance to the **Public Market** which sells top quality food. Displayed on the stalls are fish, vegetables, fruit and flowers, fresh every day.*

THE PUBLIC MARKET

Since it opened in 1979 in a huge old industrial warehouse, Granville Island's Public Market has become a veritable institution. Locals, as well as those who come to shop from more distant parts of town, are able to find all kinds of specialities here, from fresh vegetables to fish and shell fish straight from the sea, from the exotic spices needed for ethnic cuisine, to rare imported wines, from fresh pasta to over 150 different types of cheese. Although the building and setting are those of a traditional covered market, more European in style than the modern American commercial centres, the Public Market is, in fact, more like a treasure trove for gourmets and a well stocked bazaar, than any normal agricultural foodmarket. There is indeed quite a difference for, alongside the peppers and prawns, one finds stalls selling attractive craft articles, such

as ceramics, glassware, carved items, dried flower arrangements and even jewellery, all made in the numerous craft workshops on Granville Island. During the summer months the artists work outside in the street and are one of the island's tourist attractions. While a visit to the market is obligatory for finding natural and fresh ingredients, or special, imported goods, one shouldn't forget another important commercial enterprise on Granville Island. **Kids Only**, situated at the entrance to the area, on the opposite side of the island to the public market, is dedicated entirely to children.

Delightful hand-crafted toys for youngsters are sold here and parents will find themselves reaching for their wallets quite happily. Outside there is even a water park with slides and games where children can play and have fun.

*The modern façade of the **Emily Carr College of Art and Design**.*

*On **Granville Island**, as well as a ride along the seafront, you can enjoy all kinds of cabaret and musical entertainment performed by street artists.*

THE ART SCHOOL

It is obvious that the art school should be located in what could be described as Vancouver's Montmartre. It is named after **Emily Carr**, the painter born in Victoria on Vancouver Island in 1890. Emily Carr alternated her studies in San Francisco, London and Paris with long periods living with the Indians of British Columbia and Alaska, constantly accompanied however, by her personal zoo which, apart from the usual cats and dogs, included a monkey, parrots and a white mouse called Susie. Emily Carr is a supreme example of the character of the people of British Columbia; identifying culturally with Europe, they are also deeply conscious of their unspoilt natural environment and the native primitive cultures, both of which clearly influence art and everyday life. The presence of many painters' studios, and a romantic (and extremely expensive) village of **houseboats** near the Art School, complete the bohemian atmosphere of the area.

ENTERTAINMENT

Granville Island has a wonderfully artistic atmosphere, due not only to the fact that many artists have their studios and display their works here, but also to the presence of the **Arts Club Theatre**, where both famous classic works and new experimental and avant garde pieces are performed.
However, the most immediately characteristic feature of the area is the presence of groups of **musicians, buskers, mimers, acrobats and street artists** on almost every corner and in many of the cafés too, some of which organize their own programme of concerts. At the **Granville Island Brewing Company** one can watch beer being made according to the Bavarian Law on Purity of 1516, which is almost a performance in itself given the awesome care devoted to its production.

FALSE CREEK

BURRARD STREET BRIDGE

False Creek owes its name to an error made during a reconnaissance carried out by the Royal Navy when originally charting the area. Most probably it seemed to be an outlet of the **Fraser** delta which meets the Pacific just slightly further south, or a larger channel like Burrard Inlet. The mistake was quickly discovered when the explorers ascent of the 'creek' ended after only five kilometres.

The navy's cartographers, however, had already written the word 'creek' while waiting to give it a name and, instead of cancelling it, scribbled *false* alongside. The name stuck, despite the local authorities who, in 1891, presented a petition to have the name changed to the more appealing 'Pleasant Inlet'. For many years the creek was not of great importance and indeed the only way of crossing it was by Indian canoe. The eastern end was, however, gradu-

ally filled in to create more space for the heavy industrial plants there and today in fact False Creek is reduced to only three kilometres in length. When Vancouver began to extend to the south, the continual need to skirt around the far end of False Creek became increasingly inconvenient and finally in 1932 **Burrard Street Bridge** was built near the mouth of the inlet. Thus Burrard Street with its bridge crosses the entire city centre as far as the port, where Canada Place now is, and provides a speedy link for the south side of the city. The bridge has a central steel span, typical of the engineering of the period, and entering it one passes beneath elegant arches built in Art Déco style at both ends.

The south side of False Creek did not develop greatly until the 1970's and '80's, when a modern district came into being there, named after the stretch of sea.

*An aerial view of **False Creek** showing Granville Street Bridge and, behind it, Burrard Street Bridge.*

*The central span of **Burrard Street Bridge**. Opened in 1932, its piers have Art Déco style arches on top.*

THE MARITIME MUSEUM

The Maritime Museum is a simple 'A' shaped building where the legendary ketch, the *St. Roch* is housed. This two-masted sailing ship, 140 feet long (approximately 43 metres) belonged to the corps of mounted police who became famous in the 1930's and '40's for being the first to navigate the Arctic waters of the Northwest Passage in both directions. In the 1950's the same corps completely circumnavigated the North American continent.

HERITAGE HARBOUR

Heritage Harbour is situated where False Creek flows into English Bay, in front of the Maritime Museum. Moored in this little harbour are perfectly restored period sailing vessels. Enthusiasts can appreciate the highly skilled manual building techniques and enjoy the aesthetic pleasure of seeing boats which were built as unique and individual pieces.

The Maritime Museum, known as the **St Roch National Historic Site** *and the* **Heritage Harbour** *with historic vessels.*

*Peaceful and well-organized, from **Vanier Park** there is a magnificent view across to **West Vancouver** and the mountains behind.*

VANIER PARK

Situated between the southern entrance to Burrard Street Bridge and **Kitsilano** beach, Vanier Park has many interesting facilities. As well as the Maritime Museum and the Heritage Harbour, there are the **Planetarium**, the **Observatory**, the **Vancouver Archives**, the **Academy of Music** and the **Vancouver Museum**, where Indian artifacts are displayed and scenes and buildings from pioneering days are reproduced. Every May, the **Children's Festival** is held here and all summer the park is filled with youngsters as, with a continuous breeze off English Bay, it is the ideal place to fly kites. In fact, this sport is enjoyed by many enthusiasts who have long left childhood behind them and one can often watch veritable competitions of skill take place between somewhat grown-up kite fliers.

H.R. MacMILLAN PLANETARIUM

According to Indian legend, the entrance to the bay is guarded by a crab, and the **Planetarium**, suitably shaped like a flying saucer, is guarded by an enormous metal crab, a sculpture by George Norris. On the dome of the building inside, one can survey the heavens from any latitude and at any time in the past, present or future. The building also houses the **Vancouver Museum**.

BC PLACE STADIUM

The home of the local football team, the **B.C. Lions**, is at the eastern end of False Creek and here the largest **air-supported domed structure** in the world stands, covering an area of 4 hectares. It was built in 1982, in preparation for the Expo and was Canada's first covered stadium. The teflon roof is supported by the pressure of sixteen rotating propellors. As well as football, concerts, horse shows and other entertainment are held in the stadium.

*The fountain with the statue of the **crab**, one of the most popular monuments in Vancouver. Behind, looking like a flying saucer, is the **Planetarium**.*

*An aerial view and a detail of the **B.C. Place Stadium** with its unusual roof.*

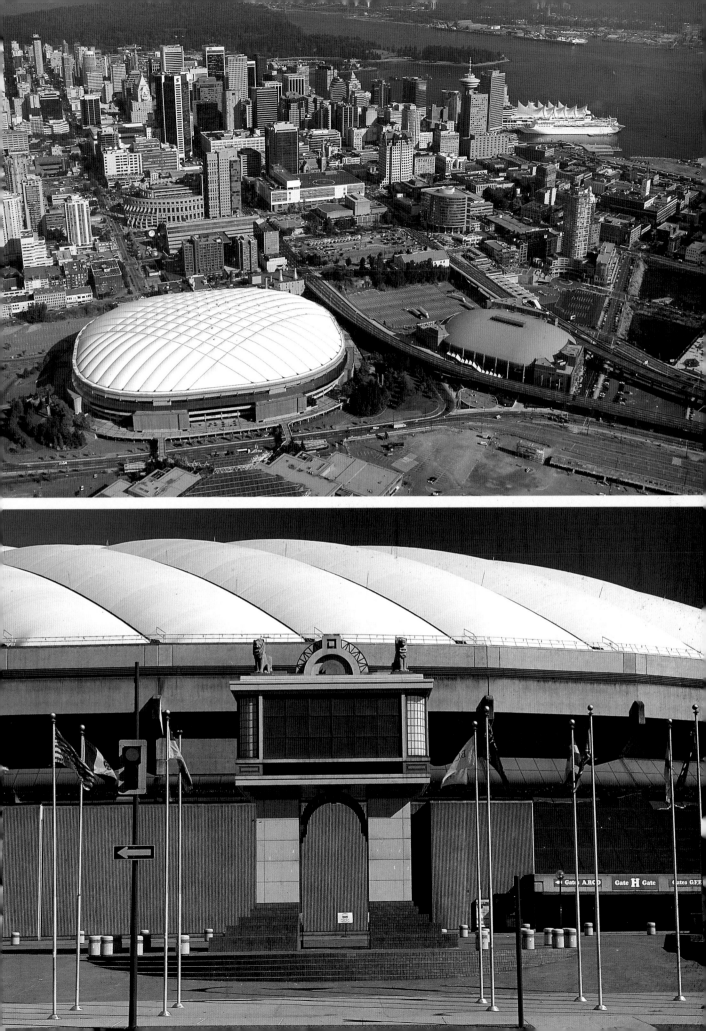

SCIENCE WORLD

Near B.C. Place Stadium, on the eastern shore of False Creek, is Science World. Built as one of the major pavilions for Expo '86, it was altered and extended to re-open as Science World in May 1989. Science World British Columbia is a non-profit making community organization which stimulates the curiousity, creativity and thrill of learning by encouraging the exploration of the arts, science and technology.

This splendid geodesic dome rests on 182 pillars and is 155 feet high. The exterior of the building consists of 766 panels of stainless steel sheathing and has 391 lights. The interior of the building is an immense 10,220 square metres altogether, with the **Alcan Omnimax Theatre** at the top. This incredible theatre, which seats 400 people, features all-round sound and a screen which is equal to five sthreys in height. The showing of a 45 minute Omnimax film requires over four kilometres of film. This wonderful centre offers the ultimate experience in hands-on entertainment with light, sound, games and gadgets. The exhibits change constantly so that every visit is a new experience.

*Different views of the geodesic dome on False Creek which was built for Expo '86 and now houses **Science World**.*

CITY HALL

On the corner of Cambie Street and 12th Avenue, amidst family houses and little parks, Vancouver's City Hall rises lofty and splendid. The building represents something more to the city than an administrative centre; it is somehow emblematic of Vancouver's determination to become a modern city, leaving behind the hard times and dark days. Indeed, after the **great fire** of 1886 which almost totally destroyed the young city of Vancouver, the new seat of the city hall was a tent immediately erected in Stanley Park as proof of the city's resolve to rebuild. The present City Hall was built in the 1930's, in the middle of the **Depression** which severely damaged the local economy, and it became a symbol of the vitality and courage of a city determined to celebrate its first fifty years. At the time, about 40,000 people, a sixth of the population, were living beneath subsistence level and the most common everyday sight were lineups for bread in front of the public welfare centers.

Nevertheless, the city persevered with the building of its Hall and special measures were taken to finance it. In 1936, fifty years after the founding of the city, the building was completed, admirably simple and pure in design, architecturally a mix of modern Neoclassic and Art Déco. In front of the main entrance, a statue of **George Vancouver** lends an additional air of sobriety, even if no one is actually sure that it really is George. As with the monument to Gassy Jack for which an old photo of an unidentified man standing on a chair was used, so a dusty painting portraying a gentleman in 18th-century dress, possibly Charles Vancouver, the brother of George, was used as the model for the accepted founder of the city.

The clock tower of Vancouver's **City Hall**.

*The futuristic dome of the **Bloedel Conservatory** gleaming in the sun and surrounded by magnificent flower beds in **Queen Elizabeth Park**.*

QUEEN ELIZABETH PARK
&
BLOEDEL CONSERVATORY

The park was opened in 1912 on a small hill known as the **Little Mountain**. At 150 metres, this is the highest point in Vancouver and from here one can enjoy a magnificent all-round view of the entire city. Originally, there was a basalt quarry on the site and from here the cobbles used to pave the streets of Vancouver were obtained, up until 1908.

Today, a delightful **arboretum** flourishes where the quarry once was, and elegant little ponds have been made from the old watersheds. It was named **Queen Elizabeth Park** in 1940 after the visit of King George VI and Queen Elizabeth, but work was only completed in 1961. Paths, fountains and waterfalls were made and, with its Japanese gardens and numerous flowerbeds, this is one of the favourite places for picnics and weddings pictures.

Other attractions in the park are the tennis courts, golf course and a field for cricket, not to mention the chance of having a free view of the baseball games in the **Nat Bailey Stadium** below. A sculpture by **Henry Moore**, entitled *Knife Edge* is another point of interest in the park.

In 1969, the **Bloedel Conservatory** was also added and its futuristic design anticipated many of those structures later built for Expo '86. Inside the hothouse, brightly coloured birds fly freely and in the specially recreated habitat over five hundred species of tropical flowers and plants are kept.

Queen Elizabeth Park is attractively set out with flower-beds and perfectly kept lawns in the style of an English garden. Inside the *Bloedel Conservatory*, though, parrots and other tropical birds fly around in the heady perfume of tropical flowers in the recreated jungle and desert environments.

VanDUSEN BOTANICAL GARDENS

On what was once an elegant golf course, the VanDusen Botanical Gardens, opened in 1975, now house one of the most famous collections of plants in the world. Over 6,500 kinds of plants from all the continents flower throughout the seasons providing a continual show of colour. Although intended for research and educational purposes, there are also some entertaining features, such as the **labyrinth** made from one thousand cedars, and the **Festival of Lights**, an evening performance held during December.

UNIVERSITY OF B.C.

Although all the buildings were not finished until many years later, the first students arrived in 1915 (and now the largest University of B.C. is Canada's third university). The campus, on **Point Grey** on the Strait of Georgia, is a mixture of architectural styles, though these are harmonized by the surrounding trees and gardens. The university now has twelve faculties, nine schools of specialization and twelve research centres, as well as Canada's second largest library.

*In the **VanDusen Botanical Gardens** there are over 6,500 different species of plants.*

*The entrance to the **UBC** library and the **Clock Tower**.*

*The unusual building housing the **Museum of Anthropology** is surrounded by totem poles representing both the religion and the artistic creativity of the tribes of British Columbia's **First Nation**. The museum exhibits artifacts belonging to this 6,000 year-old culture.*

MUSEUM OF ANTHROPOLOGY

The Museum of Anthropology was designed by the architect **Arthur Erikson**, responsible for many of the most innovative public buildings in Vancouver such as the **Law Courts** and **Simon Fraser University**, inspired by the traditional style of Northwest coastal Indian building. The museum emphasizes the grandeur and complex nature of the indigenous cultures, almost completely eliminated by the European immigrants.

The building opened in 1976 in the university area and is mainly dedicated to the Salish, Bella Bella, Haida, Tsimshian, Tlingit, Kwakiutl and Nootka Indian cultures. Displayed are the various structures found in Indian villages, original totem poles dating from the end of the 19th century, crockery, ritual masks and jewellery, as well as many common, everyday utensils and a large collection of photographs which help

the visitor better understand the complex culture of the American Indians.

The artist, **Bill Reid**, a sculptor and goldsmith of Haida origin, born in 1920, played an important role in the creation of the museum as consultant and supervisor. He worked for the University of British Columbia from 1958-1962 collecting, classifying and arranging everything necessary for the reconstruction of a traditional Indian village. One of his most famous sculptures, **'The Crow and the First Man'**, representing the Haida legend of the creation of the world, is displayed in the museum.

Further emphasizing the variety of cultures one finds in Vancouver, not far from here is the **Nitobe Memorial Garden**, a most beautiful Japanese garden designed by the architect Kannosuki Mori in 1960 using plants specially imported from Japan.

The vast swimming pool and sports facilities on **Kitsilano Beach.**

Excellent facilities and entertainment, as well as sea and sun, have made **Kitsilano** *one of the most desirable residential areas.*

KITSILANO BEACH

Kitsilano Beach perhaps provides the best example of Vancouver's hedonistic culture; this is the ideal place to fully enjoy a healthy open-air life-style. In the summertime thousands of tanned bodies enjoy the enormous seawater **pool**, sports fields and centres and the long sandy beach, in defiance of Vancouver's reputation of being a rainy city. Kitsilano is also the name of the residential district which, with its private family houses, has maintained its original peaceful atmosphere. There are also many attractive cafés and restaurants here providing a pleasant backdrop for those who have come to enjoy the sea and sun. The relaxed atmosphere has encouraged many shops and businesses to open here recently, in preference to central Vancouver, now considered to be too 'metropolitan'.

BURNABY MOUNTAIN

To the east of Vancouver is the **Burnaby Mountain Conservation Area**. A village has been completely reconstructed here, and forms an open-air museum of the history of Vancouver in the period between 1890 and 1925. The **Burnaby Village Museum** consists of over thirty buildings and the staff, dressed in period costume, recreate the daily life of a frontier town in the early days of its development. Thus, for example, alongside the blacksmith is a typical old emporium and a Chinese spice shop where the friendly, talkative staff describe a normal working day in the business, portraying the life of the visitors' great-grandparents down to the smallest detail. The museum is surrounded by a park full of rhododendrons and at the highest viewpoint stands a collection of **carved wooden poles**, like modern, stylized totems.

*The carved poles on **Burnaby Mountain** from where one can enjoy a complete panorama of Vancouver.*

*The modern buildings of **Simon Fraser University** designed by architects Erikson and Massey. Situated on Burnaby Mountain, it opened in 1965.*

SIMON FRASER UNIVERSITY

The Simon Fraser University is within the **Burnaby Mountain Conservation Area**, situated on the top of the mountain at a height of 350 metres, overlooking the city. The university opened in 1965 and is named after the explorer who, in 1808, ascended the river, also named after him, on which Vancouver stands. The choice of its decentralised position on the furthest eastern side of **Greater Vancouver** is representative of the intention of the first rector, Gordon Shrum, to break away from traditional academia. At the time of its opening, the university consisted of the normal, classic humanitarian and scientific faculties, but innovative directions in research and teaching quickly emerged.

Simon Fraser is, for example, one of the few universities to have a department of advanced studies in **criminolo-gy**. Another unusual feature for a Canadian university, generally more similar in style to the English and Europeans than the Americans, was the introduction of grants for sportsmen and women in the 1960's. As a result, Simon Fraser University excels in basketball, football, athletics, swimming and soccer with teams on the same competitve level as the most famous American colleges.

The university also has a well known art gallery and a museum of archaeology and ethnology, both of which are open to the public.

The main university building is itself a work of art and has received praise and awards internationally. An elegant, heterogeneous structure in steel, glass and cement, it was designed by the architects Arthur Erikson and Geoffrey Massey.

Most of the Indian totems near to **Capilano Suspension Bridge** are by **Chief Mathias Joe Capilano** and his wife, **Mary.** They represent Indian gods, such as the **Thunderbird** (below).

CAPILANO SUSPENSION BRIDGE

The areas of **North** and **West Vancouver** lie on the northern shore of Burrard Inlet and are connected to the rest of the city by **Lions Gate Bridge, Second Narrows Bridge** and the **Seabus**. The most distinctive features of the area are the majestic **Lions Mountains** - after which the bridge is named - and the three peaks of **Grouse, Seymour** and **Cypress Mountains**, moody and changeable, but always impressive whether covered with snow, wrapped in mist or hidden by low, dark cloud. The two areas at first developed quite independently from the rest of Vancouver and have, in fact, very different characters: North Vancouver is an industrial port while West Vancouver is a stylish district with an English atmosphere. They are separated by the **Capilano Canyon**, created by the Capilano river. It is an exciting experience to cross the canyon by the **Capilano Suspension Bridge**, a narrow, swinging footbridge, 137 metres long and 70 metres above the luxuriant vegetation of the canyon and the river below. The first bridge, consisting simply of taut rope cables, was made in 1889. The present structure was built in the 1950's and consists of steel cable, anchored at both ends by 13 tons of cement.

During the 1930's the Indians developed the custom of placing totem poles near the bridge. Many of the first totems were made by **Chief Mathias Joe Capilano** and his wife **Mary** while the statues in red cedar portraying Indians, are the work of two Danes, Aage Madsen and Karl Hansen, who managed to eke out a living during the Depression sculpting these figures. One of the most popular attractions of the area is the cosy and picturesque **Tea House**, which opened in 1911 serving refreshments to the already numerous visitors and soon also added a market selling Indian goods and articles.

*The historic **Tea House** where, as well as refreshments, Indian crafts are sold.*

*On the following pages: the **Capilano Suspension Bridge.***

*The **Lonsdale Quay Market**, in the port of North Vancouver, sells all kinds of goods from fruit to fish. With its cafés, restaurants and even a hotel it is almost a miniature city set within the port itself.*

LONSDALE QUAY MARKET

The handiest way to reach **North Vancouver** is without doubt by the **Seabus** which crosses Burrard Inlet every 15 minutes. The crossing is pleasant as well as practical: it costs much less than a taxi, you avoid rush hour traffic jams on the bridges and you can enjoy the sea breeze and a wonderful view of Vancouver. On the whole, the port of North Vancouver is precisely that - cluttered wharfs, cranes, hoists and merchant ships at dock, all of little interest to the tourist. On the quay where the Seabus arrives however, there is a huge commercial centre known as the **Lonsdale Quay Market.** The market, which opened in 1986, sells goods of all kinds, from agricultural produce such as fresh fruit and vegetables, to fish, lobster, oysters and meat, but also imported food specialities, and even jewellery and fashion clothing elegantly displayed in little shops in balconies above. Cafés and good restaurants are plentiful and there is a hotel on the upper level.

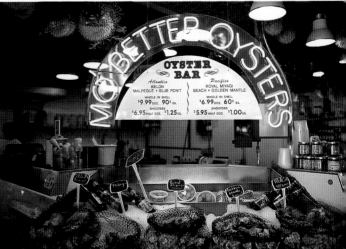

*The panorama from the **Grouse Mountain cable car** is quite stunning.*

GROUSE MOUNTAIN

Just half an hour from downtown centre is Grouse Mountain, one of the main ski resorts of the area. In the winter months thousands of people come here every day to enjoy the unusual opportunity of excellent skiing so close to the centre of a maritime city. The mountain remained without a name until 1894 when a climbing party came across a grouse on its slopes and decided to name the peak after the wild bird, rather than any particular physical feature. The mountain's popularity dates from 1924 when an enterprising businessman built a toll road leading almost to the summit. The magnificent panorama enjoyed from the road quickly made Grouse Mountain one of the favourite spots to visit on the West Coast. The resort has excellent downhill slopes and cross-country runs, some of which are also open at night and, clearly visible from the city centre, this is one of the most characteristic features of the north shore in

trip lasts barely five minutes and on a clear day from the summit, at 1,250 metres, one can enjoy the vast panorama sweeping from Vancouver Island 80 kilometres away, to the San Juan Islands almost 200 kilometres to the south in the state of Washington in the USA. Consequently, Grouse Mountain is one of the most popular resorts in summer too, when, as well as the excellent bars and restaurants, one can visit the **Theatre in the Sky**, which opened in 1990 and is now one of Vancouver's favourite attractions. There is also a large playground where children can play at living like real pioneers in houses, a little fort and various other buildings made from tree trunks, in this wild and natural setting.

LIGHTHOUSE PARK

A lighthouse at the furthest point of **West Vancouver**, Point Atkinson, has given its name to one of the most attractive parks in this area of the city. From here there is a panorama over the entire bay and city of Vancouver while the **Strait of Georgia** and **Vancouver Island** are visible looking towards the west. The park offers many walks amidst the luxuriant vegetation of this northern rain forest.

*From a clearing in the luxuriant vegetation on **Point Atkinson**, the lighthouse after which the park is named, overlooks the Strait of Georgia.*

wintertime; skiing on the floodlit slopes with the bright lights of the city and of the ships in the bay immediately at one's feet is indeed a unique experience. The neighbouring peaks, Seymour and Cypress, also have good ski slopes, but only Grouse Mountain is equipped to host international events. The first two-chair ski lift began operating here in 1949 and the largest cable car in North America was opened in 1965. Its capacity was doubled in 1976 with the **Superskyride**; capable of carrying one hundred people, it rises in a breathtakingly steep climb almost from sea level to a height of 1,130 metres. The

*Ferries arrive and depart for **Nanaimo**, the **Sunshine Coast** and **Bowen Island** from the charming port of **Horseshoe Bay**.*

HORSESHOE BAY

Horseshoe Bay and the village of the same name lie beyond Burrard Inlet on the shores of **Howe Sound**, a bay on the coast to the north of West Vancouver. The twisting **Marine Drive** follows the coast passing through beautiful green countryside and some of the most exclusive residential areas of West Vancouver. This charming seaside village, with a mere one thousand inhabitants, nestles amidst the verdant hills which run down to the water's edge. This tranquil beauty spot with a pretty tourist harbour and inviting cafés and restaurants was known to the Indians as Chai-hai, a term indicating the gentle sound of thousands of little fish as they leap out of the water. Visitors might wish to do no more than relax, lulled by this soft sound, but from Horseshoe Bay, ferries also arrive and depart for **Nanaimo** on Vancouver Island and for the **Sunshine Coast** and **Bowen Island**. The Sunshine Coast, for example, is a peninsula to the north, past Howe Sound, famous for its low rainfall and a popular residence for artists; for a modest sum one can buy a ticket, leave with the morning ferry, tour the coast by car, and return with the ferry in the evening. One has plenty of time to visit Horseshoe Bay while waiting for the boat which leaves every hour. At the far end of Howe Sound another interesting town to visit is **Squamish**. Even more interesting is the means of transport: from North Vancouver one can take the last **steam train** in Canada, the **Royal Hudson** which peacefully puffs around the entire coast of Howe Sound, providing its passengers with not only the pleasure of bygone travel, but also magnificent views.